When Unknown Is Known

Sakthi

First Published in 2021

Becomeshakespeare.com

One Point Six Technologies Pvt Ltd

123, Building J2, Shram Seva Premises,
Wadala Truck Depot, Wadala (East),
Mumbai 400037, India

T: +91 8080226699

Wordit Art Fund helps deserving authors publish their work by providing monetary support. To apply for funding, please visit us at www.BecomeShakespeare.com

ISBN - 978-93-5438-661-9

To all my teachers

To all my friends

Table of Contents

Presence 9

You are the onion 11

I didn't know 12

We are not different 15

No other light 20

When 23

Maya..26

Nature 31

If we left..33

Season..34

Soul 36

Yet to be seen 38

Space has..40

Schooling 43

Seeds and potter 44

First step 47

Learning 48

Well being 50

Teaching 52

Writing 55

Flowering 56

Writing 59

Poem 64

Essence 66

Society 69

Hurry Up 70

Hero worship 73

Warfare 76

Survival 79

Serious 82

News are 85

Table of Contents

Life   89

Selfie 90

Asha 93

Pointing 95

Travel.. 97

Affair 100

8

I

Presence

You are the onion

You are the onion,
you let Life peel layers and
layers of you slowly
showing you what you are holding,
As an onion it is an intense
process to go through

at the same time

You feel lighter
as you are being peeled,
your longing to see your innermost core
increases day by day
as it can only hold the space
for the intensity to dissolve and disperse
into Nothing.

I didn't know

I didn't know
I came so close to you

We met only few times
Very brief talks
Moments of eye to eye to contact

But
I didn't know
I came so close to you

Until you left
From my world completely
Without any notice

Left with no clue
Felt helpless
Not knowing
What to do

Where to go

I did all that
I can do
Never knew that
I came so close to you

It is a bond
Not from this life time
It goes beyond time
It goes beyond ages
It goes beyond eons

Bond
Is always there
Here or there
It is always there
Past or Future
It is always there

Our closeness
Is not of moments
We shared together

Closeness is
Always close
But we tend to lose

So
The unrest of missing you
So
The feeling of getting lost
Though I search you
Very far
You are always
So close

But I have no clue that
I came so close to you.

We are not different

Are we?

Have you ever noticed
Same thing
Saying by
Different
People
But
With
Slightly
Different words
Different voices

We are not different
Are we?.

Essence is same
Flavours are different
Colours of

Appearance

Music of

Tones

Choice of

Words

May

Differ

But

Essence is same

We are not different

Are we?.

Have you ever seen

Trees that

Choose

Same

Colour

Leaves?

If thats so

We are not looking

Closely

When you

Close

To

Trees

It

Shows

It's

Vibrant colours

The shades

And

Hues of

Green

That blends

And

Varies with

Colours

Of

Every

Season

In

Season

Summer

Or

Monsoon

It is

Never

Ever

Same

Though it's

Essence is same

We are not different

Are we?.

Then where we have

Gone

Wrong?.

We are saying

Same thing

With

Slightly

Different words

Different voices

To know the answer

We have to

Look

Closely

We are not different

Are we?.

No other light

No mans land

You are

Neither

This

Nor

That

You are

Neither

Black

Nor

White

You can see

Neither

Light

Nor

Dark

Long

Tunnel

That stretches

Very long

You are a

Traveller for

Very long

Like a

Firefly

That

Forgot it's

Known

Path

Now

It has to discover

New path

No other guiding light

Except it's own light

Dark tunnel is

Very scary

You can see a light

Very far

But

You

Don't know

How far

No choice of

Going

Back

That

You come

So far

Other end

May be so far

Like a

Star

No other light

Except it's own light

No other light

Except it's own light

When

When
Unknown is
Known

You see the beauty
In ugliness

Perfection in
imperfection

Order in
Disorder

You hear the silence
behind the noise

You feel choice less
Is the best choice

You know not knowing
Is the true knowing

Inaction
Is the right action

Uncertain is
Very certain

Completeness in
Work in progress

In progress is the
Real progress

When unknown is
Known

You see

Presence in
Absence

Stillness in
Movement

Emptiness in
Fullness

When unknown is
Known

You sense

Timelessness behind
The time

Past and future
In the Now

When unknown is known

Paradox
makes
Perfect sense

Maya

Is this world

Is

Maya

Or

Is it

Real

Or between

The two

White lilies

That blossoms

In quietness

Of the winter night

Knows the secret

In that silence

Laughter of

Fireflies

Holds

The answer

27

Vast night sky

And

The sparkling stars

Lives

The meaning of answers

Human being

Can know the answer

And be the answer

But how?.

Are you willing to

Embrace everything

All

That is within

You

And

Around

You

Like a puppy

That barks

And plays

With you

Like a

Sweet heart

Are you ready to

Listen to your

Sweet

Heart

That

Embrace

Your emotions

Your turmoils

Your churnings

And

Let your

Heart

Beat

You

Like Heartbeat

In Shock

Shake all of you
Stir all of you
And let
Love of
Heart
Bring everything to the
Surface

Face all that happens
Then you can
Sleep like a baby
Or like a puppy
With little smile
On face

In that sleep
When you smile
Is it neither
Dreamy sleep
Or
Smiley life

Sleep like a baby little by little

Then you know the answer

What

Lilies of winter night

Laughing fireflies

Smiling stars in dark night sky

Known for timeless times

II

Nature

If we left

Noon breeze

Dancing leaves

Chirping birds

Standing trees

Quietness of Afternoon

In cool shade

Sitting on park bench

Writing a poem

Life is blessing

If left alone

If we left

Life

Alone

Season

Winter night
Summer morning
Autumn evening
Spring noon

Every morning is
Spring
Every noon is
Summer
Every evening is
Autumn
Every night is
Winter

Every night is
Winter
Every evening is
Autumn
Every noon is

Summer
Every morning is
Spring

Spring noon
Summer morning
Winter night
Autumn evening

Soul

Being in a
Garden
Is like
Being in a
Grove

Being in a grove
Is like
Being in a
Forest

Being in a forest
Is like
Being a
Tree
Being a
Grass
Being a
Bird

Being a
Soil
Being a
Soul of the
Forest

Soul of the
Forest is
Soul of the
Garden

Soul of the
Garden is
Soul of the
Forest

So you can be in a forest
While in a garden
So you can own a forest
While you own a garden

Yet to be seen

In the early morning hours
Staying close to
Wilderness

Staying close to
Closeness of wilderness

Staying quite to quietness
To feel the
Silence beneath the silence

Silence beneath the silence is
Silent
Silent
Space behind the sky is
Yet to be seen
In the quite early morning hours
But
Sky is full of stars

That is glowing in stillness

Silence beneath the silence is

Silent

Silent

Space behind the sky is

Yet to be seen

In the quite early morning hours

But

Sky is full of stars

That is glowing in stillness

Space has

Are

You

A

Milk

Man?

Or a

Milky man?

Are you

A

Passenger

Or

Spaceship?.

Are you

A

Passenger

Of

Spaceship?

Spaceship

Travels

In

Space

Space

Has

Space

For

Milkman

Milky man

Spaceship

And

Space

Space

Has

Space

For

Space

Space

Has

Space

For

Space

III

Schooling

Seeds and potter

Four walls of class room

Confining children to

A

Room

Like growing

Banyan tree in

A pot

Pot maker makes

Pot with his own design

Does that fit

All seeds in

Classroom

Each seed is unique

Though they grow

Together

If they put up in

Same pot

Same room

Is there a room

For their expression

Freedom of expression

Never comes with freedom

It is confined to classroom

It is confined to potter design

Does potter aware of his own design?

Patterns in design?.

The more potter look at his own

Design

Closely

The closer

He knows the seeds

Seeds and potter are not

Different

In fact potter needs seeds

To sell his pots

But seeds never need potter

It can grow wildly

Because

Seed already has design

Within itself

For the fullest expression

No one can

Take away

Seeds freedom

Potter can delay with his

Pot design

When potter seeks

Freedom

Seeds show the way

Let potter free himself first

Then he can design pot for

The seeds

Seeds never in need of potter

But the potter is

First step

First step in teaching is
To understand
How learning happens

First step to understand
How learning happens is
To be the learner

First step to be the learner is
To be the observer

First step to be the observer is
To step back and watch

First step to be the observer is
To step back and watch

Learning

Learning in
The world
Is it
Child driven
Or
Adult driven?

If it is
Child driven
Learning happens
Naturally

If it is
Adult driven
Learning happens
Unnaturally

Naturally

The child is

Curious

Playful

Adventurous

And much more

Unnaturally

The adult is

Dull

Boring

Repetition of old

And much less

Which one do you choose

Child driven

Or

Adult driven

Self driven

Or

Society driven

Well being

Interest of social well being
Comes with interest?
Or under compulsion?

Well being
Ever
Comes
Under compulsion?

Under compulsion
Interest comes?
Or
Disinterest comes?

Under compulsion
Interest comes?
Or
Disinterest comes?

Disinterest comes

When well being

Is not in interest

Disinterest comes

When well being

Is not in interest

Teaching

Teaching

Is

To

Learn

How

To

Teach

Learn

How

To

Teach

By

Learning in

Teaching

Every

Learning

In

Teaching

Is

To

Teach

How

To

Teach

You

Learn

To

Teach

By

Learning

In

Teaching

You

Learn

How

To

Teach

Teaching

By

Learning the

Learning

In

Teaching

IV

Writing

Flowering

Reading
A
Poem
Like
A
Being
With
A
Flower

You
Can't
See
The
Flower
If
You
Are
In

A

Rush

As

You

Pass by

Fragrance

Invites

You

To

See

The

Flowering

To

See

The

Flowering

Be

There

As

A

Witnessing
Presence

In
Your
Presence
Flowering
Happens
Slowly
In
You
Flowering
Happens
Slowly

Writing

My friend
Asked 'Me'
Where
Do you
Locate
Yourself
In
Your
Writing

I
Can't
Locate
Myself
In
My writing

Writing
Writes

Itself

Writer

Is

Just

A

Pen

Characteristics

Of

Pen

May

Express in

Writing

But

It is

Not a

Pen's

Writing

Writing

Writes

Itself

As if
There is
No
Writer

Writer is
There
But
He is
Not
There

As Hafiz said
"I'm a
Hole
In
A
Flute
Life
Breaths
Moves

Through.

Listen

To

This

Music"

Flute

Also

Listen

To

The

Music

As

It is

Being

Played

Hard

To

Express

This

Process

Writing

Process

Writing

Writes

Itself

Writing

Writes

Itself

Process

Poem

Poem blends
And transforms
Brings something
Fresh
Which remains
Forever fresh

Poem is like a river
It has its rhythm
It has its pattern
It is flowing
In stillness
It is still
While flowing
Stillness is flowing

Poem makes you feel
Divine ness within
And

Divine ness in

Everything you see

65

You see

Essence

Poetry is

Painting

With

Pen

With pen

Paint

What

You

See

And

Also

What

You don't

See

Essence of

Beauty

Essence of

Bounty

Essence of

Essence

Sense

Your

Essence

Essence in

All

Your

Sense

When

You

Sense

Essence in

All

Sense

Essence

Sense

Your

Essence

Essence
Sense it's
Essence

V
Society

Hurry Up

Hurry up

Hurry up

Time is

Running

Out

Hurry up

Hurry up

Time is

Running

Out

Where are

We

Going

I tell you

Later

Hurry up

Hurry up

Time

Is

Running

Out

Running for

What?

I tell

You

Later

You always

Tell

Later

Later

Also

You tell

Later

Latter

Now

It is
Late

Late for?
Not to be
Late

Why late?

Don't want to be
Late
I want to
Be ahead

Ahead for?

To go ahead

For what?

Not to be late
To go
Ahead

Hero worship

Popular

Hero

He is

So

Popular that

Everybody

Knows

Him

Very well

He is

So

Popular

Because

He

Acts

Sings

Dances

Fights

Does

Same

Action

Repeatedly

In his

All

Movies

Content

May

Be

Different

But

Format

Is

Same

Hero

Worship

Never stops

Until

One

Realise

Hero is zero

He is
Just a
Projection
On
Screen

Without
Screen
Without
Light
He is zero

If we don't make
Zero a
Hero

Hero becomes
Zero

Hero becomes
Zero

Warfare

War is
Fair?.

War has
Fare
We
Pay
Huge
Fare

But
We
Never
Care

We
All
Like
War

Between

Nations

Region

Religion

Relation

Above

All

Has

Strong

Reason

Reason

Is

To

See

Who

Is

Strong

You   Vs   Me

Us   Vs   Them

Me   Vs   Me

War

Is

Mind

Set

It

Is

Already

Well

Set

If

We

Don't

Reset

We

Won't

Be

There

To

Reset

Survival

Survival

Of

The

Fittest

The

Fittest

One

Survives

We all

Need to

Compete with

Each

Other

To

Be

Fit

One

Who is

Unfit

Don't

Survive

So

We all

Need to

Compete with

Each

Other

Each Vs Other

Each Vs Other

No

One

Is

Fit

For

Ever

No one is

Fit

Forever

Forever to see

Who is fit

Fittest

Goes on

Forever

If It

Goes on

Forever

Nothing

Survives

Ever

No thing

Survives

Ever

Serious

Are
You
Serious
About
Life

Life
Needs to be
Dealt with
Lot of
Seriousness

Without
Seriousness
You can't
Achieve
Anything

Without

Seriousness

You'll be

One of the

Losers

Don't

Lose

Your

Seriousness

Be

Serious

About

Seriousness

Be

Serious

About

Being

Serious

Being

Serious

Is

Very

Serious

So

Be

Very

Very

Serious

Be

Very

Very

Serious

Else

Serious

Lose it's

Seriousness

Life

Lose it's

Seriousness

Serious

Seriousness

News are

Our

News are

Our

News exchanges are

Movies

Of

Movies

Well

Cut

Edited

In

Pre and post

Production

Pre and post

Production

Produces

Movies

Of

Movies

Movies

Of

Movies

Always

Produce

More

Movies

Of

Movies

Movies

Of

Movies

Always

Produce

More

Movies

Of

Movies

More

Movies

Of

Movies

Produce

More

And

More

Movies

Of

Movies

More

Movies

Of

Movies

Produce

More

And

More

Movies

Of

Movies

VI
Life

Selfie

If
You
Take
Photo of
Yourself
By yourself
For yourself
It is a
Selfie

Look
Pose
Feel
The
Same way

Same way
You
Take

Selfie

Different
Faces
Different
Poses
For
Different
Selfie
To show
Your
Uniqueness

Uniqueness
Falls into
Unique
Pattern

Pattern
Is same
Selfies are
Different

Pattern

Is same

Selfies are

Different

Asha

Godman
Offers
Free
Flight
To
Kailasha

Flight
To
Kailasha
To
Free
From
Our
Asha

With
Asha
We go

To
Kailasha

Godmans Offer
Free flight to
Kailasha
To free our
Asha

With asha
We go to
Kailasha

Pointing

Finger

Pointing

To

The

Moon

Finger

Pointing

The

Moon

Pointing

The

Moon

Moon

Pointing the

Pointing

Finger

Pointing

Finger

Points

Pointing

Finger

Pointing

Finger

Points

Pointing

Finger

Travel

Plan
For
A
Travel

Either
It is a
Planned
Travel
Or
Unplanned
Travel

There
Is
A
Plan
For the
Travel

So

Plan

For a

Travel

As

You

Travel

Travel

Has

Plans

For

Your

Travel

As

You

Travel

Travel

Has

Plans

For

Your

Travel

So you

Travel

As if

You

Plan the

Plans of

Travel's

Travel

Plan

So you

Travel

As if

You

Plan the

Plans of

Travel's

Travel

Plan

Affair

Worldly
Marriage
Is a
Grand
Affair

Grand
Costumes
Makeups
Decorations
Entertainments
For
Entertaining
The grand
Affair

Entertaining the
Grand
Affair

Is a

Quite

An affair

Grand

Affair

Is not

A

Quite

Affair

Quite

Affair

Is a

Quite

An

Affair

Quite

Affair

Is a

Quite

An

Affair

An

Affair